DENVER
BRONCOS

BY JOSH ANDERSON

Stride

An Imprint of The Child's World®
childsworld.com

Published by The Child's World®
800-599-READ • www.childsworld.com

Copyright © 2023 by The Child's World®
All rights reserved. No part of this book may be reproduced or utilized in any form of by any means without written permission from the publisher.

Photography Credits
Cover: © Dustin Bradford / Stringer / Getty Images; page 1: © Africa Studio / Shutterstock; page 3: © Trask Smith/Cal Sport Media / Newscom; page 5: © Doug Pensinger / Staff / Getty Images; page 6: © Rick Stewart / Stringer / Getty Images; page 9: © Al Bello / Staff / Getty Images; page 10: © Dustin Bradford / Stringer / Getty Images; page 11: © stevezmina1 / Getty Images; page 12: © Matthew Stockman / Staff / Getty Images; page 12: © Sean M. Haffey / Staff / Getty Images; page 13: © Matthew Stockman / Staff / Getty Images; page 13: © Dustin Bradford / Stringer / Getty Images; page 14: © Ezra Shaw / Staff / Getty Images; page 15: © Doug Pensinger / Staff / Getty Images; page 16: © Steve Dykes / Stringer / Getty Images; page 16: © Brian Bahr / Staff / Getty Images; page 17: © Jeff Zelevansky / Stringer / Getty Images; page 17: © Jed Jacobsohn / Staff / Getty Images; page 18: © Rick Stewart / Stringer / Getty Images; page 18: © Rick Stewart / Stringer / Getty Images; page 19: © Vincent Laforet / Staff / Getty Images; page 19: © Harry How / Staff / Getty Images; page 20: © Justin Edmonds / Stringer / Getty Images; page 20: © Gregory Shamus / Staff / Getty Images; page 21: © Joe Scarnici / Stringer / Getty Images; page 21: © Dustin Bradford / Stringer / Getty Images; page 22: © Lutz Bongarts / Staff / Getty Images; page 23: © Jeff Gross / Staff / Getty Images; page 23: © stevezmina1 / Getty Images; page 25: © Andy Lyons / Staff / Getty Images; page 26: © Donald Miralle / Staff / Getty Images; page 29: © John Grieshop / Stringer / Getty Images

ISBN Information
9781503857704 (Reinforced Library Binding)
9781503860476 (Portable Document Format)
9781503861831 (Online Multi-user eBook)
9781503863194 (Electronic Publication)

LCCN 2021952624

Printed in the United States of America

TABLE OF CONTENTS

Go Broncos! 4
Becoming the Broncos 6
By the Numbers 8
Game Day 10
Uniform 12
Team Spirit 14
Heroes of History 16
Big Days 18
Modern-Day Marvels 20
The GOAT 22
The Big Game 24
Amazing Feats 26
All-Time Best 28

Glossary 30
Find Our More 31
Index and About the Author 32

GO BRONCOS!

The Denver Broncos compete in the National Football **League's** (NFL's) American Football Conference (AFC). They play in the AFC West **division**, along with the Las Vegas Raiders, Kansas City Chiefs, and Los Angeles Chargers. Fans in Denver have been lucky enough to root on two of the best quarterbacks ever: John Elway and Peyton Manning. Denver last won the **Super Bowl** in 2015. Let's learn more about the Broncos!

AFC WEST DIVISION

Denver Broncos

Kansas City Chiefs

Las Vegas Raiders

Los Angeles Chargers

PEYTON MANNING WAS SKILLED AT CHANGING THE OFFENSIVE PLAY BASED ON HOW THE DEFENSE LINED UP AGAINST HIM.

BECOMING THE BRONCOS

The Broncos played their first season of football in 1960. The team was part of the American Football League (AFL). Denver and nine other AFL teams joined the NFL in 1970. The other three teams in the Broncos' **division** also come from the AFL. Before the team began play, it needed a name. The team owners held a name-the-team contest. Fans gave their suggestions for what the team could be called. The name "Broncos" was the winner.

THE BRONCOS DID NOT HAVE A WINNING SEASON DURING THEIR TEN YEARS IN THE AFL, BUT MANY MEMORABLE PLAYERS TOOK THE FIELD IN A BRONCOS UNIFORM DURING THAT TIME.

BY THE NUMBERS

The Denver Broncos have won the Super Bowl **THREE** times.

14 regular season victories in 1998— a team record!

606 points scored by the Broncos in 2013—an NFL record!

The Broncos have won **15** AFC West division titles.

Fans and players were ecstatic after the Broncos won Super Bowl 50.

EMPOWER FIELD AT MILE HIGH OPENED IN 2001. IT REPLACED THE BRONCOS' OLD STADIUM, WHICH WAS CALLED MILE HIGH STADIUM.

GAME DAY

The Broncos play their home games in Denver, Colorado. Their **stadium** is called Empower Field at Mile High. The city of Denver is located approximately one mile (5,280 feet) above sea level. No other NFL team plays at such a high elevation. Air becomes less dense at high altitudes. The Broncos hold the second-highest home winning percentage in NFL history (.686). Many people think this is because opponents have trouble breathing in Denver's "thin air."

We're Famous!

You can usually find Broncos players on Bryant Street, where Empower Field is located. But in 1998, running back Terrell Davis traveled to *Sesame Street!* The All-Pro speedster hung out with Telly Monster, Elmo, and Baby Bear on the PBS television show. The Muppets wanted to congratulate Davis on a recent victory!

UNIFORM

ORANGE

WHITE

Truly Weird

The Broncos once played a game without any quarterbacks! With every QB unavailable, the Broncos used a backup wide receiver at the position. Kendall Hinton played quarterback in college. He used that experience to lead the Broncos in a game against the New Orleans Saints in 2020. Hinton only threw nine passes all day. The Broncos lost 31–3.

Alternate Jersey

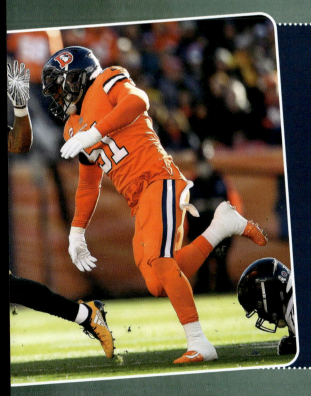

Sometimes teams wear an alternate jersey that is different from their home and away jerseys. It might be a bright color or have a unique theme. The Broncos wore these all-orange uniforms, with an alternate helmet, for a December 2020 game against the Bills. Unfortunately, Denver lost to Buffalo 48–19.

THUNDER LEADS THE TEAM AND COACHES INTO THE STADIUM BEFORE EVERY HOME GAME.

TEAM SPIRIT

Going to a Broncos game at Mile High is a blast! There's one fan tradition that's meant to really get under the opponents' skin. Every time a rival misses a pass, the crowd starts a chant of "IN-COM-PLETE." The Denver Broncos Cheerleaders wear Western-themed uniforms and root on the team at every game. The exciting atmosphere also includes two different mascots. Thunder, a live Arabian horse, has been entertaining fans at the stadium since 1993. Miles is a costumed Bronco who makes over 300 appearances around Denver each year. You can even invite Miles to your birthday party!

MILES

HEROES OF HISTORY

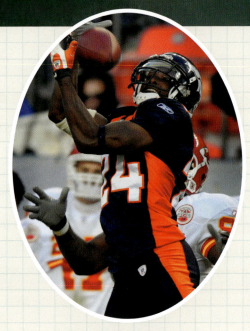

Champ Bailey
Cornerback | 2004–2013

Known as a "shutdown cornerback," Bailey anchored Denver's defense for almost a decade. In 2019, he became the first defensive player in Broncos history to enter the Pro Football **Hall of Fame**. Bailey is the NFL's all-time leader in passes defended with 203.

Terrell Davis
Running Back | 1995–2001

Davis is the Broncos all-time leading rusher. He finished his career with 7,607 yards and 60 rushing **touchdowns**. "T. D." led Denver to two Super Bowl victories in a row. Davis was the **Most Valuable Player** (MVP) of Super Bowl 32. In 2017, he was elected to the Pro Football Hall of Fame.

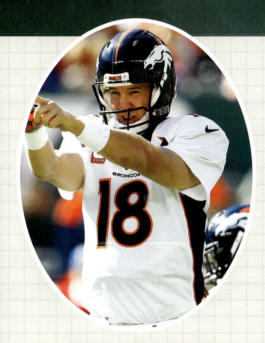

Peyton Manning
Quarterback | 2012–2015

Although Manning only played four seasons in Denver, he made a huge impact. Manning led the Broncos to the Super Bowl twice. Behind Manning, the Broncos won Super Bowl 50 in 2016. In 2013, Manning set the NFL single season record for touchdown passes when he threw 55!

Shannon Sharpe
Tight End | 1990–1999, 2002–2003

Sharpe's 8,439 receiving yards for the team are the third most of any Bronco. He was chosen for eight career **Pro Bowls** and won two Super Bowls with the team. Sharpe was elected to the Pro Football Hall of Fame in 2011.

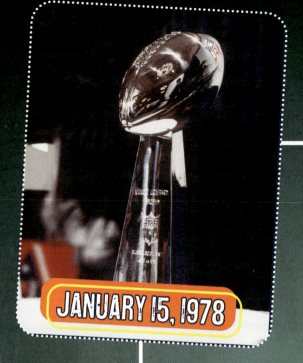

JANUARY 15, 1978

The Broncos make it to the Super Bowl for the first time. Fans are thrilled, even though Denver loses to the Dallas Cowboys 27–10.

The Broncos make a trade with the Baltimore Colts and receive number one draft pick John Elway. Elway would lead the franchise for many years.

MAY 2, 1983

BIG DAYS

JANUARY 31, 1999

John Elway plays his final game. Denver defeats the Atlanta Falcons 34–19 to win its second straight Super Bowl.

The NFL's best defense leads the Broncos to victory in Super Bowl 50. The 24–10 win over the Carolina Panthers is the final game in Peyton Manning's career.

FEBRUARY 7, 2016

MODERN-DAY MARVELS

Justin Simmons
Safety | Debut: 2016

After snatching five interceptions during the 2020 season, Simmons was named a Pro Bowler for the first time. Simmons was rewarded for his strong play. He signed a four-year contract that made him one of the highest-paid safeties in the league entering the 2021 season.

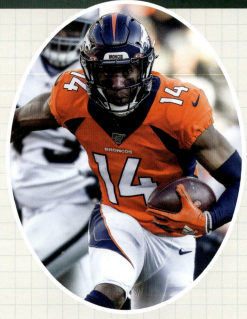

Courtland Sutton
Wide Receiver | Debut: 2018

After being selected in the second round of the NFL Draft, Sutton set the league on fire. He had more receiving yards (1,816) and touchdowns (ten) in his first two seasons than any Bronco in history. Sadly, Sutton missed most of 2020 with an injury. He returned for the 2021 season and totaled 776 receiving yards.

Javonte Williams
Running Back | Debut: 2021

Williams scored 22 touchdowns in his junior season at the University of North Carolina. After that, the Broncos picked him in the second round of the NFL Draft in 2021. Williams scored his first NFL touchdown in his third game as a pro. He led the team with 1,219 yards from scrimmage as a rookie in 2021.

Russell Wilson
Quarterback | Debut: 2022

Wilson was traded to the Broncos before the 2022 season. Before that, he played 10 seasons for the Seahawks and led the team to a winning record nine times. His 292 touchdowns rank 15th all-time. He's been chosen for the Pro Bowl nine times.

BEFORE HIS RECORD-BREAKING CAREER IN THE NFL, JOHN ELWAY WAS A STAR AT STANFORD UNIVERSITY.

THE GOAT
GREATEST OF ALL TIME

JOHN ELWAY

In 16 years as the team's quarterback, Elway led the Broncos to five Super Bowls. He's considered one of the best to ever play his position. Elway completed 4,123 passes for 51,475 yards with 300 touchdowns during his career. The nine-time Pro Bowler retired after winning the MVP Award in Super Bowl 33. After his playing career, Elway was hired as the Broncos' General Manager of Football Operations in 2011.

FAN FAVORITE
Tim Tebow–Quarterback
2010–2011

Tebow was already one of the most popular players in football when he was drafted. He won the Heisman Trophy while at the University of Florida. As Denver's starting quarterback in 2011, Tebow led the team to the **playoffs**. Tebow and his teammates defeated the Pittsburgh Steelers 29–23 in the wild-card round

THE BIG GAME

JANUARY 25, 1998 – SUPER BOWL 32

Entering the 1997 season, John Elway had taken the Broncos to the Super Bowl three times. But each time, Denver lost the big game. At 37 years old, Elway's career would soon be coming to an end. Time was running out for the franchise's best player to earn the Broncos their first Super Bowl victory. Behind three touchdowns by Terrell Davis, the Broncos came out winners in Super Bowl 32. The 31–24 victory over the Green Bay Packers brought Denver its first NFL championship.

Teams that win the Super Bowl receive the Vince Lombardi Trophy, named for the coach who won the first-ever Super Bowl in 1967.

HEAD COACH MIKE SHANAHAN LED THE BRONCOS TO 138 REGULAR-SEASON VICTORIES AND TWO SUPER BOWL WINS.

AMAZING FEATS

23 Touchdowns — In 1998 by RUNNING BACK Terrell Davis

395 Field Goals — Made by KICKER Jason Elam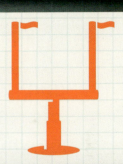

849 Career Catches — By WIDE RECEIVER Rod Smith

1,038 Solo Tackles — For SAFETY Dennis Smith

ALL-TIME BEST

PASSING YARDS
John Elway
51,475
Peyton Manning
17,112
Craig Morton
11,895

RUSHING YARDS
Terrell Davis
7,607
Floyd Little
6,323
Sammy Winder
5,427

RECEIVING YARDS
Rod Smith
11,389
Demaryius Thomas
9,055
Shannon Sharpe
8,439

SACKS**
Von Miller
110.5
Simon Fletcher
97.5
Karl Mecklenburg
79

SCORING
Jason Elam
1,786
Brandon McManus
837*
Jim Turner
742

INTERCEPTIONS
Steve Foley
44
Austin Gonsoulin
43
Billy Thompson
40

*as of 2021
**unofficial before 1982

DEMARYIUS THOMAS HOLDS 16 TEAM RECORDS WITH THE BRONCOS, INCLUDING 1,619 RECEIVING YARDS IN A REGULAR SEASON.

GLOSSARY

division (dih-VIZSH-un): a group of teams within the NFL who play each other more frequently and compete for the best record

Hall of Fame (HALL of FAYM): a museum in Canton, Ohio, that honors the best players in NFL history

league (LEEG): an organization of sports teams that compete against each other

Most Valuable Player (MOHST VAL-yuh-bul PLAY-uhr): a yearly award given to the top player in the NFL

playoffs (PLAY-ahfs): a series of games after the regular season that decides which two teams play in the Super Bowl

Pro Bowl (PRO BOWL): the NFL's All-Star game where the best players in the league compete

rookie (RUH-kee): a player playing in his first season

sack (SAK): when a quarterback is tackled behind the line of scrimmage before he can throw the ball

stadium (STAY-dee-uhm): a building with a field and seats for fans where teams play

Super Bowl (SOO-puhr BOWL): the championship game of the NFL, played between the winners of the AFC and the NFC

touchdown (TUTCH-down): a play in which the ball is brought into the other team's end zone, resulting in six points

FIND OUT MORE

IN THE LIBRARY

Bulgar, Beth and Mark Bechtel. *My First Book of Football.* New York, NY: Time Inc. Books, 2015.

Jacobs, Greg. *The Everything Kids' Football Book, 7th Edition.* Avon, MA: Adams Media, 2021.

Sports Illustrated Kids. *The Greatest Football Teams of All Time.* New York, NY: Time Inc. Books, 2018.

Wyner, Zach. *Denver Broncos.* New York, NY: AV2, 2020.

ON THE WEB

Visit our website for links about the Denver Broncos:
childsworld.com/links

Note to parents, teachers, and librarians: We routinely verify our web links to make sure they are safe and active sites. Encourage your readers to check them out!

INDEX

American Football Conference (AFC) 4, 8

American Football League (AFL) 7

Bailey, Champ 16

Davis, Terrell 11, 16, 24, 27–28

Denver, Colorado 4, 7–8, 11, 13, 15–19, 23–24

Elway, John 4, 18–19, 22–24, 28

Empower Field at Mile High 10–11, 15

Hinton, Kindell 13

Manning, Peyton 4–5, 17, 19, 28

Miles 15

Shanahan, Mike 26

Sharpe, Shannon 17, 28

Simmons, Justin 20

Sutton, Courtland 20

Tebow, Tim 23

Thunder 14–15

Williams, Javonte 21

Wilson, Russell 21

ABOUT THE AUTHOR

Josh Anderson has published over 50 books for children and young adults. His two boys are the greatest joys in his life. Hobbies include coaching his sons in youth basketball, no-holds-barred games of Apples to Apples, and taking long family walks. His favorite NFL team is a secret he'll never share!